MYSTERIOSOS
AND OTHER POEMS

ALSO BY MICHAEL McCLURE

POETRY
Hymns to Saint Geryon
Ghost Tantras
Little Odes
Organism
September Blackberries
Jaguar Skies
Antechamber
Fragments of Perseus
Selected Poems
Rebel Lions
Simple Eyes
Rain Mirror
*Three Poems (Dolphin Skull, Rare Angel,
and Dark Brown)*
*Huge Dreams (The New Book / A Book
of Torture and Star)*
*Touching the Edge: Dharma Devotions
from the Hummingbird Sangha*
Plum Stones

NOVELS
The Mad Club
The Adept

PLAYS
The Blossom
The Mammals
The Beard
Gargoyle Cartoons
*The Grabbing
of the Fairy Gorf*
Josephine the Mouse Singer
VKTMS

ESSAYS
Meat Science Essays
Scratching the Beat Surface
Specks
Testa Coda
Lighting the Corners

COLLABORATIVE
"Mercedes Benz," with Janis Joplin
Mandala Book, with Bruce Conner
*Freewheelin Frank, Secretary of the
Angels: As Told to Michael McClure*
by Frank Reynolds
Lie, Stand, Sit, Be Still
with Robert Graham

CD & DVD
Love Lion (video & CD)
with Ray Manzarek
The Third Mind (DVD)
with Ray Manzarek
There's a Word (CD) with Ray Manzarek
I Like Your Eyes Liberty (CD)
with Terry Riley
Rock Drill (2 CDs)
Abstract Alchemist (DVD bio)
Rebel Roar (DVD)
Touching the Edge (DVD)

MYSTERIOSOS
AND OTHER POEMS

MICHAEL McCLURE

A New Directions Book

Some of these poems appeared in *American Poetry Review, Golden Handcuffs, Beatitude, Transit, Avenue Be, Miami Sun Post, War and Peace, Saxifrage, Beat Scene, Zyzzyva,* and *Café Review,* and online in *Big Bridge, MiPOesias, Otoliths,* and *Litkicks.* Others have been published in broadsides by Palace of Governors Press, Santa Fe, NM; Moe's Books, Berkeley, CA; and Tangram Press, Berkeley, CA.

Manufactured in the United States of America
First published as a New Directions Paperbook (NDP1171) in 2010
Published simultaneously in Canada by Penguin Books Canada Limited
New Directions Books are printed on acid-free paper.
Design by Erik Rieselbach

Library of Congress Cataloging-in-Publication Date
McClure, Michael.
Mysteriosos and other poems / Michael McClure.
p. cm.
"A New Directions book."
ISBN 978-0-8112-1842-9 (pbk. : alk. paper)
I. Title.
PS3563.A262M97 2010
811'.54—dc22

2009046989

10 9 8 7 6 5 4 3 2 1

New Directions Books are published for James Laughlin
by New Directions Publishing Corporation,
80 Eighth Avenue, New York 10011

CONTENTS

… Again and again.

Worm like an ideology, he eats of the core.
Aphids, like retractions, devour.
Grass, bush or tree in flower
　　　serves as reminder.

-wind, old theme of the poem,　step to step
　　　　　　　　dance to
the rewinding measures
　　　　　the fresh shoots of war.

　　　　　　　　　　— Robert Duncan

… Pluck thou my flower Oothoon the mild
another flower shall spring …

　　　　　　　　　　—William Blake

AUTHOR'S INTRODUCTION

Mysteriosos and Other Poems are remembrances, discoveries, experiences, and imaginings. In writing them I became open to unexpected shifts, to slipping through time, and to moving through once-closed moments. Our unending war against nature is the crisis from which I write. My poetry demands the tearing down of what we are and letting our energies and bodies of meat and nothingness rebuild themselves.

We human mammals hate and love that we are gorgeously out of control and also so compressed into distracted and pained social shapes. But there is alchemy, and long ago Friedrich Schlegel said, "All poetry should become science and all science become art. Poetry and philosophy should be made one."

A poem is a porthole of consciousness and experience, whether opening to the feeling of blood pulsing in the wrist, or the taste of a red-black cherry, or the sound of a rock being placed on a table.

In 1965, Francis Crick asked to use some lines from my "Peyote Poem" in his book recounting the story of the DNA discovery. It followed that Crick and I became friends and over the years we enjoyed our walking and talking. Like Crick I believe that flesh and consciousness are one thing — and I see there is no wall between biology and poetry.

While Crick was dying I wrote a poem in his honor, "Double Moire for Francis Crick." I worked with an earlier poem for him titled "Moire" and used each line to begin a stanza in the new enlarged poem. Like an organism, "Double Moire" began to be free in time and place, and to exist in the oneness of everything. In the action of writing, this poem was present in all moments: in the Ice Age, in the rings of Saturn, in deep space, and in the smallest semi-living particles at the bottoms of streams, as well as in the towers of buildings visible across the Bay. Writing it felt like a small miracle; but Walt Whitman said, "A mouse is miracle enough to stagger sextillions of infidels."

In the title section, "Mysteriosos," partitions that separate biology, poetry, and sense experience are removed and reveal shapes and births among remembered gestures and new experiences. In "Mysterioso Ten" I stand in a field of greening grass in midwinter rain and am conscious of signals moving in all directions from root to root in the soil and its countless organisms. The lines from a poem that Robert Duncan dedicated to me came to mind.

RE-

> *-turn.   In spring-up green freshet*
> *turn.   Delight to the eye,   spring*
> *to torso,   hand spring to wheel,...*

The rain became monumental and proportionless — I felt pliant and myriad-minded, and sensed sugars of the earth turning under the loam where the neighborhood deer had been walking in the night. This moment morphs into an airplane flight and then I am on a beach, in a favorite place near the Mayan ruins in Tulum, Yucatán. There are high green waves and an osprey flies in low circles, screaming, while I hold a handful of sand and see faces on the grains. The synaptic tracery of my nervous system coheres with the moment. Life goes on like this.

In "Something of India," which opens this collection, I am crossing the International Date Line in a plane which is a pinpoint of the mindless fossil-fuel ambition to subdue Nature — so that I may visit an enclosed garden, where butterfly flocks fly from rock walls to pools and rest on flowered branches.... A few days later in an Indian forest we are charged by an enraged elephant who suddenly recognizes an old human friend among us and turns back into the trees, trumpeting and shaking her head and massive ears as her anger subsides. Later there is a huge paw print of a tiger in the lake mud: two outstretched hands can fit within it. Some things of India.

"Dear Being" is a garland of thirty-seven poems that are born from earlier books, repeating opening lines of poems to begin new poems. Exploring buddhist *hua yen* thought led "Dear Being" through some of the ways in which nature intermingles with our flesh and our memories. "Dear Being" is a means to speak of my age, my love, my pleasures, my fears ... and that I long to be a brother of Blake, Shelley, Su Tung-p'o, Emily Dickinson, and drunken Anacreon — as well as the jellyfish in the surf and the eagle that nests over the coastal ridge not far from here.

Michael McClure

MYSTERIOSOS

AND OTHER POEMS

SOMETHING
OF INDIA

CROSSING THE INTERNATIONAL DATE LINE BY AIR

I'M BLACK, BLACK IN MY CORE
THOUGH ONE EYE OF LIGHT
peers inside of me.

THE WAVES OF BLACKNESS
E
N
T
E
R
and return
in the same instant.

The blackness inside a salmon
or a root of peyote.

My shudders are decency and indecency
interpenetrating
like wisdom and compassion.
LIBERATION IS
ONE
SINGLE
FREEDOM,
or not,
it is not moving pictures
not big-time sports
not the technicolor terrorism
of consumption
on the glittering screen
in front of me
on the back of the seat ahead.

*

DANCING ON SNAKES' HEADS
MOVING
through
my
life
in
these
airports.

*

E
V
E
R
Y
BEING
is a babe
on death row
even the worms building
missiles.

THE BUTTERFLY GARDEN
IN KUALA LUMPUR

MY
SLOW-FLAPPING
HEART
FLIES
where
floating flights
of butterflies
by the waterfall
leave
me
high.

High
in this butterfly enclosure,
I
love
you
beside me
in your green and damson sari.

SILVER BREAKERS
OF THE INDIAN OCEAN

TAGORE MIGHT HAVE BODYSURFED
on these tall silver breakers
where
frightened
ghost-white crabs
streak
for their holes
in steamy sunlight.

MANGOS AND PLASTIC

FORTUNATE TAGORE,
with his inner life of gardens
and paths
under
mangos.
My life
is eagles, and cars,
and mountains,
and plastic trash
that scatters cracked
and smiling faces.

DAMP LIPS

PLASTIC TRASH BLOWING
in the rubble
is
new
shapes
of leaves.
The heap being muzzled
by the cow's thoughtful lips
might
be
an
anthill.

LUXURY AT FISHERMAN'S COVE

WHAT NERVE IT TAKES
to realize how hideous
AND
GLORIOUS
this life
is:
life eating life,
and the lapis lazuli kingfisher
hovers
over
the
crystal
pool
as we float on a sea
of petroleum.

NAGARHOLE PARK

THIS LUMINOUS ROADBED OF RED-SILVER CLAY,
alight with the sun of India,
once performed in erotic dances
of
ancient
stars.
Our car
jogs
past dark deer
peering from the shade
of teak trees and brush
while a jungle fowl
preens his green-black tail
for his ladies.

*

THE
ELEPHANT
CHARGES,
shrieking in rage,
and our aged guide,
the Anglo-Indian colonel,
shakes one finger
out the car window.
"Stop!"
he shouts to his "old friend"
and she does
and she stares
short-sightedly
from wrinkled eye bags
AND
SHE
TURNS

AWAY
from us,
then swings back
and bellows
her jaw-shaking trumpet blast,
and shuffles
away sideways
into the swinging branches.

*

BY THE LAKE
a white-headed
eagle
glides over
as
we
sip
sugared instant coffee.

Nagarhole National Park, Karnataka

NINE ELEPHANTS

LIKE ANGELS BATHING
ears and tusks
in a deep forest pool
at
T
W
I
L
I
G
H
T,

I love you

HERE IT IS

IF STORYTELLER PADRAIC COLUM'S
CELTIC SOUL
is anywhere
it is in this forest
with this herd
of elephants eating
branches,
and the spotted deer,
and the tiger
in
the
twilight
leaving her
enormous paw print
in gray clay
of the lake bed.

WORKERS WALKING FROM
THEIR TEMPLE TO THE FIELDS

THERE IS A GARDEN OF FLOATING COLORS,
and the smell of sandalwood,
and the fragrant rice of imagination,
behind
the red and yellow dots
on their brows
after they stop for pujah
in the temple.

I imagine
damp earth, pebbles,
and the crunch of leaves
on the sensitive
soles of their feet.

SOMETHING OF INDIA
on the plane again

ROARING ON THE RUNWAY, AND BEGINNING
TO RACE
PAST THE GREEN HILLS,
with raindrops on the porthole,
I remember the sacred cow
smiling blithely
in the sweaty rush
of the evening crowd
at the Madras train station.
She adores the smell of shit
in the air
and the excitement of human mammals
coming together
in fumes
and smoky light.

Not moving pictures,
not big-time sports
not
the technicolor terror
of consumption

*

Now
uniformed women make
precise
smiling faces
on a glittery
screen
before my eyes.

Wheels lift
with a clunk.

GRAHHRS

WAR POEMS GRAHHR POEMS

These poems, "grahhrs," take their name from anger as I spoke it in 1964
in "Poisoned Wheat," a long poem against the biocidal attacks on Vietnam
and Southeast Asia. Now the maraudings are more widely spread.

SOULS
for Ernesto Cardenal

THE SOULS HAVE NO VALUE, THEY ARE FOX FURS
THAT WE DRAPE OVER WELL-FED ARMS AND SHOULDERS
BUT STILL THEY ARE HARD-EARNED AND LONG SOUGHT
BY THOSE WITH THE LUXURY AND ENERGY
TO TORMENT AND TO LOVE THEM INTO BEING!!
STILL
WE ARE WARM STONES
and we smell ourselves
in the screeching
R
A
I
N
of cluster bombs on Iraq.

SOULS HAVE NO WORTH
except as red splatters on walls and gobbets
of meat and fox furs.

YO, NOT ME!
says the lithe cherub on his skateboard
tearing open a high protein bar.

NOT ME
says the sweaty chicken
as her beak is snipped off at the factory farm.

NOT ME
says the antibiotic heaved into the pig feed
with sheep carcasses and blood-clotted paper
from slaughterhouse floors.

WHAT ARE SOULS WHEN
SMALL WARS

ARE
THE
ART FORM
OF
PRESIDENTS
?

!   !
!

grahhr

CUPS
for Lawrence Ferlinghetti

THE CUPS WE DRINK FROM ARE THE SKULLS OF ARABS
AND THIS SILK IS THE SKIN OF BABIES.
THE FROTHING ON OUR CHINS
IS NOT RABIES NOR ARE OUR FINGERNAILS
GOLDEN SCARABS.
WE'RE NORMAL HUMAN ANIMALS
AND WE ITCH LIKE SCABIES
FOR THE RAPE OF THINGS.
IT IS ORDINARY AND BEAUTIFUL
TO HAVE THE DUTY
TO TWIST AND TEASE
THE LOVELY GLIMMERING LIGHT
WE SEE IN THINGS.

Then, one day we look about
and hope to put it back inside,
where once there was fresh foam or moss.

But we've made a cross
of wings of birds and butterflies
and it cannot lift off the ground
or push into the soil.
— Where once there was a perfume smell
of mulch
now there's petroleum
stench
turned inside out,
and fingerprints of brightness
gone away.

What
will
we
say

to
all
the
singing
realms
that
try
to
rise
inside
of
us
?

grahhr

FOURTH OF JULY

COME IN BLACK ROSES — BLACK ROSES LIKE
SOME HERO'S SHOULDERS.
HEROES DROPPING BOMBS
ON DIRT TRENCHES.
TRENCHES PACKED WITH FRIGHTENED ARABS.
Flame bombs and decapitators sizzling
— Native Americans being tossed infected blankets.

Is it OK there in the fires
and columns of smoke?
Is there a rodent
chewing calcium
from a bone,
to
make
strong
babies?

A meaty chunk of skull
next to a shard
of depleted
uranium.

A tiny spark
flicks in the air

!

grahhr

MADAME SECRETARY

IN THE BEDROOM,
THEIR STARVING FACES AND BIG-SOULED EYES
SLIDE AT THE EDGES OF TELEVISION.
—WHAT MIRACLES OF FIREARMS AND MACHETES
ALLOW CHILDREN TO MORPH
INTO VEIN-BURSTING, BULGE-CHESTED HEROES
PUTTING BARE FEET
ON LAND MINES?

Now,
a fat woman,
the Secretary of Deceit,
cuddles a child amputee
to her breasts and croons
of the need
for democracy to flourish.
I AM AWED
by her demon face
as it leans out,
falling from the glass-fronted box,
and crashes with a squeak
on the floor
spreading a scarlet pool.

grahhr

THE FANATICS
—New York City, Falluja, Beirut, Timor, Baghdad, Dresden,
Nanking, Nagasaki, Ramallah, Saigon, London, Kigali—

THE BRAVE DOOR IN THE CORE OF YOUR DYING,
in the screaming
and
W
R
I
T
H
I
N
G

brave door

silent door

grahhr

VALENTINES
for Amy

THE SPOTTED APPLE'S TASTE?
Is
it
free
or
is
it
structure?

•

RAPTURE
spreads
in
the
smell
of
APPLE BLOSSOMS
but it is light
on the scale.

WEDDING
for Rona and Paul
— beginning with lines by Emily Dickinson —

THE ROBIN FOR THE CRUMB
returns no syllable
but long records the Lady's name
in Silver Chronicle —

and the dove coos out
with sparkling breast
the bridegroom's fame,

and hand in hand
toe to toe
there's nothing old or new
in all the human
mammal game.

It's played with marriage smiles
and sumptuous feasts and vows,
and champagne toasts,
with dark-tressed hair
that will change to white
in each the other's eyes.

Years will grow stronger
in their wear
and new soft footsteps
running on the stair
will join this
new-wed pair.

They will build a pedestal
from which to reach
the most distant foreparent
and the star
that shimmers
in the country sky
above the steamy pool
and cooling stream,

now it's possible
each day can have,
with smiles and tears
and kisses,
an unimagined gleam.

EPITHALAMIUM
for Kerry and Sean

PLUMB LIVES FROM MOMENT
to hour;
carve lives from week
to year.
Plume the spines with touches
and smiles;

o

b

e

y

your hearts
in whirlpool of foment.
It's time to be growing
crowns on your heads.
Erase lines from nightly beds.
It all happens
with sun and with stars.
Love
at the start of your life.

MYSTERIOSOS

MYSTERIOSO ONE

LOVELY. LOVELY AND ANCIENT AND FOXED
with rusty brown spots as the oldest
IMMORTAL PRINCESS,
or the Bodhisattva Kwannon as a simpering
and infinitely generous
OLD WHORE.

How surprised we are at what passes
in past and future
for the scent of apples.
I

M
U
S
T
know more about the skin and muscles
and the wall of stars two billion light-years long;
I
T

I
S

all
QUICK
! ! !

MYSTERIOSO TWO

HUNGER. HUNGRY. HUGE CAVERNOUS HOLE.
HOLDING TORN BEINGS IN TRANSITION.
Lives devouring the path into light
of blackness. Inside of a cricket.
A BIG SHINING FACE WITH EYES
filling the room. Roaming
without movement. Searching for food
ARISING AROUND.

Hormones, fats, and proteins
WEARING
EMERALD

G
E
N
O
M
E
S

in a boiling sea vent.

There is a cloud leopard
with a baby's face.

MYSTERIOSO THREE

HORMONES. HORMONES WITH LION FACES. EVEN
WITH WHISKERS. MANED HORMONES GRINNING,
and swimming as they swim in deltoid shoulder muscles
— as our arms beat on the warm high waves.

V
E
N
O
U
S
meat soup on a wheel.
Spinning. Splashing out walkers.
Singers. Flyers,
TINY EATERS.
Innocence
is driven by lion faces.

Dreams being flesh
in a universe of wings —
R
E
A
L
M
S

of glorious sound.

MYSTERIOSO FOUR

A CHUNK OF LAPIS. (CHUNK) HELD BY THE SILVER
ON MY WRIST. ORANGE
beads of coral. Pitted with cavities
OF AGE.
Encircling the blue-black stone flecked
WITH GOLD.

(T

h

e

m

a

g

i

c.)

THIS SCIENCE IS LOVE.
The tiniest microbe
lies adjacent to the larger.
A CHUNK
feeding and receiving
in a secret ocean.
Glowing like a new bodhisattva
and an etched line by Rembrandt.
Plain as snakes' eyes.

MYSTERIOSO FIVE

CORRUPT AND DIMPLED BY IMAGINATION.
Nothing corrupt. Perfect as a griffon by Blake. Corrupt
as a cloud of unknowing
visioned beneath the underside of the belly.
ME,
OUTSIDE OF IT RISING (while it rises)
INTO BEINGS WITH CORN FIELDS.
A REDWOOD FOREST.
ENCIRCLING A DAYDREAM
growing living fur of sables.

I

K
N
O
W

T
H
I
S

and remember old friends
living or dead for a moment.
Reflections around
MY BARE KNEES
in the stream.

MYSTERIOSO SIX

PAWS. TO ALL PAWS LIVING AND DEAD
— Nebulae glitter on claw tips by soft pink pads.
No pause to the smell of bosomy fennel
in vacant lots by crumbling
RED BRICKS
when the rain starts.
A DEER AT THE TOP OF THE HILL.
Mist and a star in his antlers.
I am here without paws. Searching
for the trillion billion senses.

•

D
I
S
P
R
O
V
E
all but imagination,
INSPIRATION,
and the reflections, and counter-reflections, of energy.
Sow bugs sleeping in cold owl burrows
dream destinies
AND FIRE.

MYSTERIOSO SEVEN

SENSE. SENSE OF THE CANDLE'S LIGHT.
SILVERY GLOW. FEATHERY STAR OF THE HALO.
Sparks flicker the fingertips. Field of creatures
nestled on the tongue. The nose. The fern.

Feel the real muscular animal power.
The sense of haunches and wrists is reason.
Reason is non sense draped
in velvet of senses
AND WHISKERS
and blood-streaming veins.
Blind till caution is shattered
like a windshield.

H
E
R
E

I
S

SOUL MAKING.

Ordinary, useless, lovely
as a beggar dying
in cold shadows
by her cardboard box.

MYSTERIOSO A

BUILD. BUILD BOLD LOVING ARMS.
Build new love. Over and over.
Boulders on the seashore.
Build with the fecal smell of the final wreckage
and roaring smoking destruction.

Morph the feared and debased
into luxury
OF CONSCIOUSNESS
as
a microbe
on a wet boot sole
in a movie theater
creates the energy of stars.

NOW
WE
ARE
EAGLES
in the realm of eagles' wings.
(NOW WE ARE AUTOMATONS
of reductionist technology.)
BUILD LIFE. BUILD DEATH. FREE OF THE WHEEL.

MYSTERIOSO B

STAND. UNDERSTAND. STAND PAT ON THE SENSES.
THE EYE SEES MORE
than the heart knows.
Stand up in the peace horrors
and decadent war.
Admit the deep power
and
your love
of torture.
THE TEASING OF FLESH.

Say, this too is a shape of love
before love.
Now it is time to choose:
"NO!
NO, TO THE HIDEOUS
LOVELINESS."
Soon I will protect
all beings
and
stand softly
with a big smile.

MYSTERIOSO EIGHT

BLACK ARISEN TO BLACK ROSES IS VOICES
BETWEEN PETALS.
The yellow centers with anthers
B
E
G
I
N

WITH BLACK.
Lonely. Sweet as honey.
Overpopulated by blossoms and petals.
Consciousness narrowly streams
like a nematode, muscularly,
between plastics and hunks
OF MANUFACTURED THOUGHT.
Through births of new hatreds
— poisonous as ever.
Greedy for ignorance
as a sitcom.

And we stretch
in this bed

touching shoulders
just as whales and mice
do.

MYSTERIOSO NINE

FORGIVE CORE OF THE MEAT. FORGIVE MEAT FLESH.
Forgive rage. Also kindness. Touch gentle
in this strange spot.
ALWAYS VISITED. THE CORE OF ALL REALMS
— of chickadees, tadpoles, living droplets, blazing minuscule
FURNACES.

A TRILLION BILLION
INSIDE
OF ANOTHER
LIKE AN ONION,

spraying heavens
that intermix

while
we
slide
through
shallow crevices.
EMOTIONS. WATERFALLS.

•

FROZEN PONDS
WITH GOLDFISH
ALIVE AND SWIMMING
IN THE BLACK WATER.
YES!—AND MUCH MORE

SING!

MYSTERIOSO TEN

GREEN GRASS IN RAIN. BLUE-GREEN EYES.
Grass calling up yellow violets. Root
notes seethe back and forth. Aligned
to the flash of no matter.
NADA
OF
GREEN SPRING
in midwinter. "Spring up
green freshet." Blue-green eyes
nourish like the storm
and horsehead cliffs.

PLIANT DIMENSIONS.
Interludes
L
A
U
G
H
while lipids turn over dancing
and thundering under deer hooves.

A HANDFUL
OF MYRIADNESS.

Finished at Tulum, Quintana Roo, Mexico

MYSTERIOSO ELEVEN

STREAM OF FACES. FACES ON SAND GRAINS
UNDER THE OSPREYS AND HIGH GREEN WAVES.
STREAM OF ROARING NEURON LACE,

S
I
L
E
N
T

as pink flowers of peyote.
Free in the preserve the soul inspires.
No beginning or end
(like a pelican gliding low over breakers
where the night will be star sparks).

M
E
A
T.

PLAIN RED MEAT,
PLAIN DULL THING. STREAMING
BULK OF DELICATE HULKING IMAGINATION
VAST AND FAR LESS AND TINIER TOO.

Tulum, Quintana Roo, Mexico

MYSTERIOSO TWELVE

ENERGY OF DARKNESS. ENERGY OF LIGHT.
Each is a speck of the other,
hallucinations of being,
when what matters is the interwarmth
of our eyes
IN
THIS
almost secret
place.

Mined out of a wall of turquoise and gold

SOFT WINGS ON OUR BROWS
ARE NOT
like the sprays of the blue-black spumes
from our foreheads.
THE NEW
BLACK COAT
is the skin of a mammal
in candlelight.

War enters on mammoth feet,
and courage and the energy of Reason respond.

MYSTERIOSO THIRTEEN

SMILE. SMILE WITH THE SOFT EDGE
OF THE MIND.
Pliant as the lip of an abalone.
Strong as the smallest worm in its harshest
and tenderly nourishing realm.
NO MIND. NO BODY. GONE. GONE.
I stroke my hands over my chest
and your buttocks
WE
SMILE
INSPIRED
by protein pleasure
and loveliness.
So solid.
We defeat presence or nothingness.
All of me and all of you
ARE
this cameo of perfection
with smooth polished edges.

THIS
IS
REALLY IT!

CAMEOS

CAMEO ONE

WE HAVE GONE
GONE. GONE
in the hole where
soul swells
into
nothing
leaving solid space
where profiles
of gods and fairies
are carved
and
finely
polished
by the clanking of trucks,
thunder-shaking
waves,
and the taste of mangos.

CAMEO TWO
for Jane

SOFT WINGS ON OUR BROWS
ARE NOT
carved from matter
like a spray
from a dolphin's
FOREHEAD.
It's a hiss of steam
from the ripples
beside our boat
where we believe
we look deep
through waves
at the cold stone bottom
reflecting
our eyes,
and a shapeless
creature
crawls
there
W
I
S
E
R
than I am.

CAMEO THREE

M
E
A
T.
PLAIN RED MEAT
is a forest of moving
GIANTS
and proportionless bay trees
are realms
of ungathered
universes.
Echoing voices
of
hunters
reflect from a wall
of stars
and
I
do not know
to be afraid.
STILL
TOO
YOUNG
among withering
wrinkles.

CAMEO FOUR

ALIGNED
to the flash of no matter.
A HANDFUL
OF MYRIADNESS
is the taste
of flesh
in a soup
or
a
KISS.
FINGERS SMELL
of the meal
long after
it
is
eaten,
and microtubules
of neurons
visit graves
of Schubert
and sparrows buried
in childhood.

—NO
NAME
FITS!

CAMEO FIVE

EMOTIONS AND WATERFALLS
S
I
N
G
in frozen ponds
and in hell realms;
beauty burrows
in the lacquer
of
PAST
AND
PRESENT
and before
and after that
the thin scarlet varnish
is assembled of sub-miniature
lightning bolts
dimmed
by
our mutual arising.

(Imagine leaning
towards freedom.)

F
E
E
L
THAT!

I live it.

CAMEO SIX

BIRTHS OF NEW HATREDS
are hideous
and more poisonous
than
ever.
They may smell sweet
like the yellow-green
orchid
opening by
the fireplace.
NOW,
THE BLACK STEEL SAFE
D
R
O
P
S
forty stories
on
the head of a child
in the redwood forest.

"Molecular odors" of hotels
and car seats

almost rule.

CAMEO SEVEN

AND WHISKERS
and blood-streaming veins
are blind till caution is shattered
THEN
THE
POOR
DEAR
MADE
SOUL

the weightless
thing
that I struggle for
L
I
F
T
S
me as wings.

IMPERMANENT
and
tasteless

and odorless
as DNA.
A moment's delight
of teddy bear arrogance
less than one tear, toe, or finger.

Hungry dimensions
from the fluttering movie of twisted ghosts.

AND IT IS INELUCTABLE THAT I LOVE YOU.

CAMEO EIGHT

MIST AND A STAR IN MY ANTLERS.
I am here without paws.
A TRILLION BILLION SENSES
float on jealousy and envy.
Old age, ignorance,
and stumbling are a miracle.
INSPIRATION smiles like a boy
in a sandbox shining
with mandalas
AND TWIGS.
Scattered among finger furrows.
A
SMOOTH
STONE
by a motorcycle
is perfect
as the clots
of wet green tea leaves
on an oak floor.

We guess that we
are streams in darkness.

CAMEO NINE

CORRUPT AS THE CLOUD OF UNKNOWING
encircling a daydream
and fresh as the faces
of dead friends,
I
GRIN
CROSSING
the stream in the darkness.
LAUGHS
AND
TEARS
ON WINGS
flutter through
one
another
and a brown moth
with messages on his dusty back roosts
flat on the white wall.
Alight with the pheromones
of his lover.
Among piano notes
of Haydn
and invisible fingers.

CAMEO TEN

THE BLUE-BLACK STONE
is encircled
by an etched line of Rembrandt
and Love is a naked science
for the tiniest microbe.
We are cloaked with the gestures
of fingers and eyes and tongue.
S
T
R
E
T
C
H
I
N
G
out momentary protein from the boundless
something and nothingness like Necessity
and the freedom not to be. I am always here
in the black and white photograph
of an old cracked mirror. Caught
in the hunger of this moment, just as the old turtle
dives in the cloudy water.

CAMEO ELEVEN

INNOCENCE DRIVEN BY LION FACES
takes to its wings and listens with furred ears
to
WINTER
MORNING
LIGHT.
The stream warbles nearby
before sunrise.
My muscles swell when rain
moves through the grass shoots.
Remember gray sand
and propeller whirr
of wind-blown palmettos
and the apple that falls
from the truck and rolls
to
drop
through the sewer grating.

THIS IS A UNIVERSE
of
realms
that we swim through
while a horse neighs.

CAMEO TWELVE

TORN BEINGS IN TRANSITION WHIRL
AT THE BOILING SEA VENT
in emerald genomes;
A CLOUD OF TOTAL LOVELINESS
R
E
D
A
C
T
S
itself
before the beginning
of eternity.
I know limitless desires
are contained only by freedom.
THIS IS NEW AND I ROAM
searching for arms
that arise around.
I

D
R
I
N
K
from the generous breasts
of nothingness
and floorboards creak
as we pry them up.

CAMEO THIRTEEN

THE SCENT OF DECAYED APPLES
in the desk drawer
is a wall of stars
and shining shimmering dust.
MOTTLED SOUNDS
M
U
S
T
SPEAK
to the bare mildewed feet
of Kwannon's ineffable hearing.
The pink plum blossoms decorating
each perfect realm
drip big raindrops
to
the
concrete sidewalk.
Shoe soles and earthworms
move through the puddles
and mud.
It is all
QUICK
while the bell rings
through the incense.

DEAR BEING

FOR AMY

"It is better to focus on the radical originality of a situation. The thought
which flows from this has a chance of being itself more original.
This is the opposite of repentance ..."

NOW I UNDERSTAND, THE SEXUAL ADDICTION
    of my young manhood
  was a CRUCIFIXION —
    glittering and lovely
          AS
an ostrich boa and smashed mirrors
      seen on acid.
Now: I am an old man with a handsome face
      and after the bloody movie full of guns and stabbings
      and helicopters, I stop at the photo booth
and in the mirror is a dog with jowls, a silver fox,
    an eagle in the whirlpool. Here's the strip of four photos:
    a sincere man with white hair and eyebrows,
      eyes almost inside-out, staring from a black Armani collar.
    Then the same man, still in front of scarlet drapes, with his eyes
      looking up into science fiction in his forehead.
    Now his head rests dazed against the side of the booth.
      In the last photo I am fully alert: JUST AS I ALWAYS AM,
        A SUICIDAL CHILD IN LOVE WITH EXPERIENCE
      RISKING ALL TO BE ONLY WITH YOU
    as the dragon world with its hundred eyes passes.

      — And I still long to be Shelley.

MY
GOD   MY GOD!

NO   MY GOD!

Don't   MY GOD!

DO
THIS

to me!

I'm an old man made of wheels of spinning flesh.
I am here! I am there! I'm a blooming apple tree,
and giant squirrel of childhood vanities.
I am desperations of longing for the touch of kindness,
I am easy to touch but my need makes me scream
and twist my face, as it ages into pits
of wrinkles. I imagine
Himalayan blackberries and striped honeybees
and the bare loves that walk naked
through life. Let me die. But let me die
back then in childhood, or young manhood,
BEFORE
THIS HEROIC, MUSCULAR, MEATLY COURAGE
to go on living.
You brought this to me.

— 3 —

"INCOMMENSURABLE
and incomprehensible are the best of poetic creation,"
the old man sings. The galaxies are a river
seen from this direction. The child knows
it is all black behind the eyes
and that flesh is a swirl,
and Goethe knows it also as he sings.
In his mind's eye is a bust of himself
scalpeled on a boulder of scarlet marble.
Oldsters and boys both desire to be super-Goethean,
as I did, swimming in string theory and the mitochondria
of mysterious beings,
distracted by the loves and treacheries,
and by fumes of the liquors of creation,
and new drugs which were clear and solid
as the touch of bodies.

NOW AT LAST I AM HERE,
loving only you with your lynx eyes
and displaying myself
as a sensual
and wrinkled crisis.

THERE
IS
JOY
IN
THE
ROOM
sometimes — and
it is the field of complex
presences.
But they evade old eyes and shift in the corners
making a stir which can barely hide
the immense, passing
passions that muscles and neurons
can no longer carry.
The most primitive one-celled creatures
are more sophisticated than my hungers.

Sometimes you must show me
silver clouds and the smell of dark dirt.

Often I am in the deepest place till
your laugh breaks the walls.

Even laughs can have teeth.

I AM A GOD WITH A HUGE FACE. Lions
and eagles pour out of my mouth. Big white
square teeth and a red-purple tongue. There are
        magenta clouds around my head and this
            is my throne room. Actors perform
            the drama of my being inside of you
        but I am not within myself, for my self
            is out there in the birdcalls
of jays, and sparrows, and red-tailed hawks,
            and even the raven over the meadow
            where the planes pass. I know it all:
        WE ARE FLESH AND THESE THINGS
            HAPPEN IN US. Yes.
        Yes, and the flesh is outside in the branches
            rubbing shoulders with the odors
            of cherry blossoms.
                I AM STILL DRUNK
            with it. (There is white hair and blotches
                on my skin, and these shoes are hooves
        made of engraved and textured plastic
                not leather or canvas.)

SOMBREROS THE COLOR OF CHILDREN'S
COOKIES. Colorlessness at the edges
of things. Radiances of blue-silver
clouds and mountain ranges
of cool white fog. I'm dressed in a black suit;
you, you are dressed
in the color of your eyes.
Over the tops of buildings the skies
lower to the concrete and there are barbells
clacking, and the handsome glint
of future ghosts in rooms of mirrors.

THESE CRUELTIES
are stuccoed on the future
in dense, clumped pigments of war tanks and lies:
while we endlessly free ourselves
from all but old age, death, ignorance,
and childhoods of hallucination.

I would rather kiss your kind hand
on the morning sheet than be as young
as the sun cups in the field
for a thousand years

Tiny white mariposa lilies brighten
a girl's cries on the radio.

VAN GOGH, DRAWING,
must have felt like this. The hunter
throws the chipped stone hand axe. Flint
and obsidian. The spirit rises from blood
AND TURNS
LIKE
a twisting column of mercury
showing faces:
the new Nazis with plump kind cheeks
and wire rim glasses slip
into plush offices, and skinheads
pursue African students
on Moscow streets while Voznesensky's
church bells ring
praising capitalist obesity. THIS IS GOOD,
IT IS DOWN TO THE FINAL TRUTHS.
It is all inside of me. I could do it all.
Capable of every corruption. Perfect
in atrocities and gentle sensual love.
I AM HERE TO SEE IT AND TO SMELL IT
AND TASTE IT. It is always inside
of me — exactly like this.

—8—

YOU ARE MY MEMORIES OF YOU
holding my hand.
I
WANT
TO
GO
ANYWHERE.
I am a flowering.
— As the withered roses are
back there in the '50s
in the dusty cruet that was a bud vase.
(Petals crumbling and odors
spreading and falling apart.)
WITH A STARRY LOVE FOR HONESTY GROWING,
EVERYTHING IS ON TIME AS IT POURS INTO ME!
Shaping myself with the mystery of a sonnet.
I am part of all!
I will kill, torture, and maim Palestine
and tease it with fire. I will
bomb the Balkans with heavy metal
and piss in the rivers and sky.
This trembling spirit is capable of everything
and will not sacrifice a millionth of a moment,
or lose one bird shadow of pleasure,
or forget the taste of apricot honey.

YOU ARE MY MEMORIES OF YOU
holding my hand.
I
WANT
TO
GO
ANYWHERE.
I am a flowering
but my teeth break off upon cellophane.
I work at swimming to keep my muscles.
The soles of my feet are as numb as Pride.
My headaches have gone dancing,
and I still have gnarled petals
that are unendingly envious
and curl with memories of arrogance.
But through it all,
all of the mess of regret in the Hour of the Wolf,
there is a straight clean spear
OF
ACTION
and the magic streaming from active protein. I LOVE IT!

MOUNTAINS OF MATTER
MADE OF STARS

and

I love it, I know the dark materials
contain the miracle of light that has nothing
behind it (nothing!), not even one white hair on a matted,
velvet plastic vest. And my young hands
reach down gently into the pit of voidness,
and of lung, and of liver cells. And they pluck out
(in an act of magic) two figures in orgasm,
and I hold them gently through
the unending moment
of their life. Who says there are wrinkles?
Who says the feelings of experience are as limited
as living elastic skin? NOT ONE KISS
IS EVER LOST! Only GUILT
and DUTY can corrupt me!
The softness of the damp skin on your thighs
under the quilt
is the instrument of sizeless focus.

NOTHING MATTERS BUT THESE LUXURIES,
and the black cat in the green field catching gophers!

BRAVE, FEARFUL, SCARED TO DEATH
   by the boredom. A fat gray kitten rolls
     on its back, sinking baby claws
       (clean thin baby claws)
         into the pink flesh
     I was once made of.
Now I am a light show at the Avalon Ballroom
     seen high on hashish,
      spinning around the four walls.
     And my giant face, with the horses, races
around the auditorium — the feedback is a rage
   of raw sound filling the ear
     with unheard words. Or, I'm lying on the velvet throw,
   in the yellow light of the sun
     that falls on grubby linoleum,
   and allowing the Goddess to summon herself
       from my perineum.
     She ascends the fleshy, dark chakras
   taking the shapes of grahhrs and unbirthed plays
     and secret sex acts of glory
       and lucent guilt!

a Bruce Conner light show

"MIND" MEANS NOTHING BUT CONSCIOUSNESS —
a rock has it and a toadstool
and a field of particles in a complex protein
as it loops, tying a knot. My mouth
with your nipple in it
is the rising of thought,
as are the apples that rot
in the drawer, inspiring Schiller.
Gold will not speak of lead,
lead will sing of the highest while
dimmed eyes count pearls.
Numb fingers take the qualities of jewels
that they shake from the worn, greasy pouch.
IT'S AN OPERA WITH LIVING BEINGS
smaller than viruses playing the tympani.
SIZELESS STORMS OF EMOTION AND CRISIS
(as rich as the smell of a pale purple rose)
go back into the nose and spread
into branches inside my ears
and burn my eyes with sudden
feelings of love for you!

THIS IS ALL A STRING OF PEARLS
with reflections of reflections in the opulent
glimmering surface of endless flaws,
making a surface
for the fingertips to touch
while remembering perfumes.
Then there is a crunch of Point Lobos dune plants
under my brown high-top shoes,
and coming over a rise
on the sand among beach pines is my father
with his alcoholic slump. No, it isn't. I'm
introduced, "Michael, this is Robinson Jeffers ..."
And I mumble something.
In his salon among
walls of books in wooden apple crates, and pastels
of Morris Graves, Kenneth Rexroth reads
a new poem in a nasal, grating voice.
With crossed eyes, and hair alight
with genius, Robert Duncan sings songs from his *Faust Foutou*.
It is exactly like the play of the dark, pouncing weasel
in the abandoned corral under the buckeye trees,
or Kenneth Patchen's bulging eyes looking down at the waves of the Bay
where seals haul up on the mud to sleep beside traffic.

YOU ARE
  everyone
    BUT
    I am nobody.
    Nobody is very large
      and powerful
  and to say I am in a dream is wrong.
    This is much less than a dream.
      Clearer than water in a mountain stream,
      caught in the sound of ice melting.
We're in a parked rent-a-car, watching wind in the pines
    while somewhere a baby smiles on a gold quilt,
      in the sun, or in an alembic, kicking his arms and legs.
        AND HE BEGINS SHRIEKING.
    I know things as I see the color of mauve
      blossoms above the green grass and oats in the field.
      ((The plane roars in my teeth.))
            Aphrodite says,
    "There is always a knife in the flowers.
    There is always a lion just beyond the firelight."
  I am the knife and the lion and the flowers
and firelight. Powerful as a sleeping fawn.

WATER BOILS IN THE BIG COPPER TUB. White sheets
will be dipped in the blueing. Wrung out in the wringer
and then hung up to dry. THE SUBSTRATE IS SO VIBRANT
that the black eyes of the doe and her dark-eyed baby
beside her, ten feet away, on a wall of red-brown earth
by the studio door, thrill me.
I am shaken by the smell in the hayloft,
and remember my child fingers breaking a pigeon egg
and the rotten smell of it. Or racing my Harley Davidson chopper
in blackness, roaring down Guerrero Street
with Kenny Goldfinger on his Triumph, stoned on combinations
of drugs, before he lost his hand
to a propeller in Mexico. Or sitting with a dear friend
at the kitchen table drinking instant coffee
as he tells me of the almost mammalian life-complexity
of a special one-celled creature, enacted without
a nervous system. That it has volition
and intelligence.
((A CAVERN OF RED
YELLOW AND GREEN CONSCIOUSNESS OPENS
AND SPEAKS TO ME.)) THESE THINGS HAVE
prepared me to see the open soul on your face.
I am almost stunned by you and I catch my breath.

INSIDE OUT LIKE A PROTEIN, the owl hoots.
Big trouble. A child is waiting. Love streams.
Wind flails the arms of the palm trees and mimosas bow.
     Everything happens at once, in one time:
azure eyelids of the lizard blink, mynah birds
        fly to the roof, and tanks blast children
          in concrete bunkers. My long hair
          and beard are beat by the air
       as we roar through the streetlights
        in the darkness of Guerrero Street. Old age
      turns inside out and memory streams
    with each discovery. Inside out,
     roars forward and backward,
       and trickles like water through roots
       of a potted shamrock. Bravado
        sets fire to the dullness
       of an invented future. Clumps
      of red-brown seaweed tear from the rocks
       in the murky surf swell,
        BUT WHAT THIS MEANS IS
         that the truth of shifting
        complexities is purest gold.

Maui

for Leslie Scalapino

BIG CLEAR LAUGHS ARE THE BEST
 and deep-seeing eyes
 looking back through the muscles
 of mastodon hunters
 out towards
 the edge of the solar system,
 and fallen white flowers in black grass
reflecting the light of the Milky Way.
 Always hungry is the best
 BUT THERE IS NO PEACE
 it is as ongoing as the taste
 of a purple cherry
 and the brindled calico
 skin of a mango,
 warm in the morning hand
 after a cold swim
 in a blue-tiled pool.
 AND I IMAGINE
 that, like a black flatworm,
I can shake away my head and swim free.

Maui

IN THE PLANE ROAR
there is the pink-tinged slate
behind the eyelids.
Below that, slender bearded men
duel with rapiers and they picnic
on a rainy beach among boulders.
One man is pierced from front
to back and he stands
with the sword through him as crimson
soaks his white shirt.
This beckons to my inner life
and calls it to slip into
the open folds of old movies
and comic books.
I will never be as free as a sea anemone
to move outward beyond substance
past the stars. Self-rebuke
will not help in my tidepool.
WHAT I HAVE GIVEN MYSELF
is this love, invented for you.

Maui

"IT DON'T MAKE SENSE BUT IT'S IMMENSE."

R
O
A
R
of the engines
through the stockinged soles
of the feet,
and clink of ice in plastic glasses,
and smell of peppery tomato juice,
with the murmur of voices in stale air.
We forget we are held aloft by the deaths
of scores of millions.
I watch your fine ankles as you walk
ahead of me in airports and I always listen
for your voice when we float in the cool
slate-blue waves. Once a large gray
butterfly passed us, flying
to a faraway island, and later
on the sand road by the mangroves,
there was a black jaguarundi cat and her kitten.

— 20 —
for Robert Creeley

SOFT TOES CURL ON THE FLOOR, PRIMATE STYLE
with gleam of varnished wood beneath them.
The garden does not sleep at night.
Depths of darkness intricately mottle
themselves in the smell of hollyhocks and jasmine.
The flashbulb snaps off and on —
again, and again, and again, right in my face.
Four pictures are shot, and there
ARE SPOTS IN FRONT
of my eyes. Now I am
an old man with freckles
on my high forehead. (Almost forgotten
is the way the wolf moves on entering
a restaurant.) Now there is no
pretense, just the bright
oranges, browns, blacks, and blues of the photos.
The lilt of coyness hides the predator's
intent sneer. Long white hair is the head
of an eagle. There is the faintest
bruise of wisdom in the bags
under my silver-ringed, dark irises.

THE CLOUD THAT RAFAEL FOUND is the rules of freedom.
Dark green shamrocks grow in a bowl where
dead friends live in dreams. Sounds of blue-black
jays screaming. YOU
ARE
THE
LAWS
THAT I WANT
to flow like water
over spongy moss
and like mercury over a wall of garnets
and yet you are solid flesh.
Delicate and pale and sleepy in the morning,
YOUR SOUL FILLS YOUR EYES.
The pain of loving you
is almost more than I can bear
and I think I will melt in a hundred emotions,
then I am saved when you see
the small black-headed bird through the window
on the deck rail. HOW
HARD THIS
IS, DEAR BEING.

All talk of consciousness is nothing
compared to this.
The anguish of age is not speakable.

for Jerome Rothenberg

HEARTACHE NEWS WITH THE TORTURED FACES
and grim boredom verging on insolence,
and a rifle slung over the shoulders.
Lines of meaningless glyphs slither past,
beneath a band of silver
ON
BLACK.
On this Memorial Day, which tiny, poor nation
will the U.S. morph into a Hell
while the lollypop dancers sing
of our sufferings and our heroics and our adoration
of the cuteness of Norman Rockwell?
The dear old nuclear commanders
drool sugar into our ears!

NEVER
BEFORE
NOT ONCE,
NOT ONE FUCKING TIME,
in a lifetime of wars, have we seen these jitterbugs
prancing on stages in front
of the National Symphony Orchestra while
the armed forces march carrying flags.

FACES
TWISTED
in pain
from the old times when love hurt
so much that it is spotlights
filled with legs and mouths
writhing.
It is like the painted scroll
where black and white Winter triumphs
because the sheer spirit of snow, wind blown
in banks, with coal-like rocks and a frozen plant
here and there, is so molded into perfection.
The hummingbirds sipping nectar at the window
envy our sensual delights
and our bed where we see out
through the translucent curtain.
When I do not melt in a crisis
there are clarities that are as fleshed
and firm and soft as muscles.
Each day it is the same you, Dear Being
(always in a different costume)
and it is my privilege to be here, hearing your laugh.

MIRO KNOWS IT IS ALL PLAY AND POLLOCK UNDER-
STANDS
the unconscious power.
CONSCIOUSNESS
RISES
UP
in an infinite shape of Baudelaire's bat wings,
ospreys over fiords, bobby-soxers,
the smell of tangerines being peeled, and a squirrel tooth
dug from a coyote scat. It's a breeze to conceive
of violets rising in microtubules of neurons,
and apricot trees, and the tiny dark fly
moving randomly
in front of this screen. How long has she waited
to say that no boddhisattva can imagine
a mind or soul or matter? And I always
LAUGH WITH YOU,
YOU ARE SO STRONG AND DELICATE.
After zazen, sitting on the black cushions,
your wise face invents endless love in me.

I AM THE ONE IT ALL HAPPENS AROUND:
coal, star clusters, time/space, and the hungers of landlords.
In the flow it is all changeless yet never the same.
Minute, gleaming pink shells, once filled
with living gray meat,
fossilized and encased in swirling marble
under my shoe soles on a stairway
in Stockholm are active in columned
structures of my cascading neurons.
This is my cortex.
"If you wish to see the buddha you must
look into your own inner
nature." This means there are dumbbell shapes
of energies and nothingness
with no beginnings. I am so glad
to be with you.
THERE
IS
EVEN
PRIDE
in sitting next to you and eating a fish taco.

LIKE A MOTH OR A HUMMINGBIRD TURNED INSIDE
OUT
in the lightning—or a small boy
bit by a coyote pup on the tip of his finger,
IT IS
all the same.
Old age or childhood, it is all renewable,
reversible, delivered with a warranty
that nothing is there in the nothingness.
NOTHINGNESS IS THE SHADOWS
OF SEXUAL PLEASURE
and the crash of motorcycles in darkness,
and the opening of orange and yellow
nasturtiums in dew on a sunny morning.
We deliver ourselves
in long breaths and short years
to cameras in airports
and on street corners. Horses prance
and snort in an old man's childhood.
IT IS A MIRACLE
how often I have seen and heard rattlesnakes
at the side of a trail through the pines.

THIS
CITY
OF
MY HEART
was once innocent as a baby and we
grew up in it. Shoe shops. Bakeries. Umbrella shops,
flotillas of bombers flying to Asia above the marching protesters.
Eyebrows of young men are as perfectly limned
as those of Massacio's angels.
Wild white wires of the old man, twist and
snake toward his eyeball
and into the lashes. I have always known
that this work is emancipation
like my softening arm muscles
and withering skin. There is the same luxury,
as a soul and a sensuous consciousness,
in freeing the poem, and inventing
NEW BEAUTIES,
like robes and stockings,
from the skin of Leviathan.
The Mouse's castle is the national temple; we shall protect it
from nuclear terrorists.

THE THORNS IN MY FINGER MAKE STARS.
The blackberry is sweet and black
and red and bitter.
Now summer begins
in
an ocean devouring itself
in reflections,
as we are consumed by dark
and blue eyes surrounding us.
There are our images in the brindled cat,
the hopes of a hungry dog,
and the defensive rage
of a snake
making her frightening bristle of sound.
Summer enters on a sled of roses:
five petals of red, white, and pink mirror
and bunch into multiple cabbages
of color. Gone is the smell
from childhood and the rose tree
with bronzy thorns by Grandpa's garage.

Listening to Ahmad Jamal

AND I OUGHT
to be scared as my skin wrinkles. The boy dreams
of Grandpa. As I get huger I become streams
stretching into shadows of memories.
We are huge figures at small doors
of caves looking into the blue
air over the hills before us.
We are temples of conscious pasts
and futures and all fantasies
that our meat creates. With these
we rub selves against what is not there
and we laugh and cry out

AND

MAKE

BEAUTIFUL SONGS

OF IMAGINATION AND WARS.

Every inch on the road, every rock
and burr under the foot is exact and real.
Half awake, you kiss me in the morning
and I love the blessing of your breath and smile.

NOW

THERE

ARE

LIONS
roaring like hormones
in my muscles
and I know we have entered a heaven
as we swim in the salty waves
and remember the bliss of this warm house
with a sculptured, gray-brown horse head
in the window and warm yellow sun
on shining floors.
What more do we ask but this
AND ALL THINGS IN PRESENT AND PAST?
Soon we will see a black jaguarundi cat
and her kitten crossing the gray road
at the edge of the mangroves,
where once the roar of the Mayans
could be heard at the sacrifice.

YOU ARE MY MEMORIES OF YOU
　　holding my hand.
　　　　　　I
　　　　WANT
　　　　　TO
　　　　　GO
on a big ship, long ago,
　　where you wore soft gloves
　　and dolphins leapt from the black water.
　　　Now my Queen holds
THE LEOPARD'S HEAD AND SHE SEES
through those eyes and those senses.

Knowing in all possible directions.

Like Isis, I will find many parts
　　　　AND
　　　PERHAPS
I WILL BUILD A TEMPLE.

Do you remember the snake slithering on the stone steps
　　　　through strangler figs?

A tire blows out in the rut and we drive on.

Sorrow is fine, delicate, and crude.

(after a tarot reading by Diane di Prima)

EAGLES SEEN ON ACID are the rules
that are broken in old poetry. The fierce eye
of imagined laws causes cherished pains.
Gliding through the cold water, I shake loose
my head, then take it and hold it.
Like leopard eyes in the hand, I sense through it.

THERE

IS

NO

STOPPING

ME

NOW.

I am as free as an agate in a sand pile.
I am always this free, this chained, this swathed
in wrinkles, and witherings, and baby's smiles.
Nothingness is the flavor
of past, present, and future. Nothingness is the scenery
of deer and galaxies, and the armature of cities.
White hair is the color of Hell and Heaven,
and the mutilated bodies under the freeway
in blue plastic huts by their shopping
NO MORE JOKES.

Solstice

RICE PADDIES ARE LOADED WITH SOULS
and the tiny sacrifices of rice, peanuts, watermelon
in woven boxes are pecked by the spotted-neck doves.
                THE WRINKLED DOLLAR
                    lying in the tray
                        is snatched
                    as mindfully, mindlessly
                as an icicle drips in a cave
— or it can be dropped in the waxed cardboard cup
        on the street corner outside of the movie
                in the lights of the marquee.
        The beggar is as visible in remembrance
                as he is in his presence but the urge
                    to Art occludes his shimmer. We are filled
with the excitement of escapes and treachery in the film.
                            Dear Being, I am thrilled
            to be with you while the auras and zigzags and flashes
        spring from us, and into us, and through us.
        Where we are there is no greater density
                OF RICHES
                than the passing experience,
                    rippling into nowhere

"GIVE WAY OR BE SMITTEN INTO NOTHINGNESS
and everlasting light." But I am here already,
the tips of my fingers give off light.
In seven league boots I step to the right
AND WALTZ TO THE LEFT.
Exchange crowns, bow, lift legs high in the dance.
The Dark Ages are here, with the bombs
and dollars of fools. No Compassion.
The concords of greed are being delivered in tanks.

But here our heater hums
in the wet chill of Summer, Dear Being.
The cat sleeps deeply on the bed
waiting for next week's sun to fall
on the square, green rock in the yard.
The doe and her fawns are driven to us
by the construction of homes
up the road.
NOW WE ARE FRIENDS
in the diminishing Peaceable Kingdom.

— 35 —

GOING
the way of all flesh,
CAUGHT IN THE ROAR OF THE PLANES
PASSING OVER
while the bronze bell rings
in the wind.
It's all the same:
nous, pneumas, psyche
are parts of the soul
AND
THEY

DO NOT
MATTER,
not where Philip Whalen has gone;
gone with forty-seven years of my friendship
into the red-white door of fire.
This is the hunger for being gone awry.

I cry in the plush chair of the big
WOODEN ROOM,
thinking, "Poor Phil," but my grief
is for myself and not him.

The cremation

NOW I SMELL MY GRANDMA AS SHE LOOKS
at me through her thick glasses.
See the curls of her hair with the gray locks
coiled in the brown. There's sweat
of ham frying and buckwheat pancakes
in the skillet on the old, black stove.
My Grandpa sets down his coffee,
stands up, and falls to die on the floor.
There are a million hearts living
in each knock of the moment.
Each out-breath is a door.
Haydn murmurs, and the red-shafted flicker
pokes his beak through the leaves
and pries in the rocks of the wall.

We sleep, Dear Being, in the morning
not even dreaming of one ton bombs
dropping on parties at weddings,
weddings in the bright
faraway mountains.
Not one ton bombs, but the fireworks of dreams
awaken us.

SUNSET COLORS OF APRICOT AND LAYERS OF BLACK
over the ocean. A puff of summer dust where
the buckeye butterfly lands.
RIGHT HERE,
right now, is a new strip
of four head shots.
I'm an old man with his face as crazed as Clint Eastwood's.
Then I'm posed with a half-smile like serious, worn-out Tarzan.
Now, head thrown back, my chin is raised forward in mock contempt.
Then, see my domed, white-haired forehead
with chin drawn back, and looking up, dark-eyed
through the brows.
Dear Being, who else but you could love me
as you love? It is utterly true that sometimes
I am clear, and mad, or frightened, or brave.
Now that I stand with you the thorns drop
from my side, and we often sit with crossed legs
in morning light in the midst of gift orchids
and the smell of incense. Dear Being,
there is nothing like you in the space
of emptiness
that follows the last out-breathing.

PHILIP LAMANTIA'S POEM
for Nancy Peters

Goodbye handsome Gongora
of San Francisco. "*I think you're the end.*
The *greatest poet of your kind.*
You are the poet's poet of the greatest
poet's poet poet," as you wrote in a poem.
You split beauty into slivers
to build the sleek ship
of state that carries ashes
and large eyes of cinnamon
and musk. After your adventures
and travel we would sit around you listening
and watching the scarlet ribbons
of your voice move in the sea-green
foam of the air. You are the model
for ten thousand generations of the poet
we believe in. And we believe still.
Now you are as solid as the wounds
of the Christos in a fiery spoon
of morphine on a morning of masses
dripping through funnels
into the first silk tent
of their alchemy,

R
REAL
A
L

LIGHT & LIFE.

Your beauty blesses you.

DOUBLE MOIRE

DOUBLE MOIRE FOR FRANCIS CRICK

THE CHANTING IN TIBET HAS NOT CEASED
— IT IS AS IMMORTAL AS MEAT —
it sings of the Middle Way.
Put out the fires in the eye
there is another style besides hatred and heat.
Let the soul go, build a pliant strong heart.

HORNS, CYMBALS, AND LIGHTNING BOLTS OVER GLACIERS,
softness of velvet under the feet.
Toes going nowhere,
nowhere to go but
halfway to freedom;
just a being, a beast, among creatures.

BEARDED SEA OTTERS CRACKING MUSSELS
ON STONES ON THEIR STOMACHS.
That's as rich as it gets in the sparkle
of waves in the rain and the sun.
There's the need to swim and to fly
but resting and playing and eating is right for the day.

COYOTES LAUGH AND PRANCE
ON POINT REYES.
No difference. No difference from the days
of the grizzlies, the same flowers reflect
their subtle florescence in morning fog.
Hear identical sharp barks and canine snickering.

REVIVE THE PLEISTOCENE
— the great Age of Mammals — crack the rings
of Saturn and bliss-out in their dust and secret tints.
On the mastodon's tusks is a hint
of genius beyond good and evil.
When all is alive everything sings the silence.

PLEISTOCENE IS NOT GLACIAL AND THERMAL
IT IS MEAT AND MAMMALIAN,
measured by pondering hoof and faint warm
claw scratch. There's no harm in the huge eating
whether it is ribbon worm in a tide pool
or wild horse under the paws of the American lion.

CRACKS IN THE SIDEWALK REFLECT
THE DISPERSION OF CLOUDS
AND AURAS OF COLOR. Breeze on muzzle and cheek
brings opening of life and dropping of shrouds.
Cracks on the rugged boulders show garnets
and gold and primitive jade. Nothing can fade.

REALITY IS A POINT, A PLATEAU, A MYSTERY.
Two sticks lean on each other
and touch where consciousness collects
on its bundles of nothingness.
There is no nada, no something to confess,
merely dancing in the Damn and the Bless.

IT MAY BE PENETRATED, and the all
of zero presented in the sparrow's scratch
to the vain, loving eyes of the small cat
peering out from beneath the branches of toyon.
A blue-gray jay wipes her chin on a board
and peers at stones slithering from the side of the cliff.

WILD FLOWERS: MAN ROOT, SEPTEMBER
BLACKBERRIES, MONKEY FLOWER.
Now the springs are drying up
foreshadowing storms of winter's hoard;
dripping rivulets stream
over dead brown moss where the green is stored.

POEMS AND PERCEPTIONS PENETRATE
THE PLATEAU.
Stones know where to fall as they go
scrambling over and under the maze
at the edge of tooth and finger.
What I hear is no end or start of the singer.

SUCCULENT GARDENS HANG ON CLIFFS;
thick fat leaves and blossoming towers
are no different from the scat of the coyote.
There's no new stuff
in the shining buildings across the Bay;
as the earth moves the sun catches all in the rays.

THE VELVET BUTTERFLY
AND THE SMILING WEASEL
are people following calm laws
in old corrals at the side of the road,
green in a glade under the trees.
Only on their surface are the laws so strange.

BENIGN VISAGES FLOATING IN AIR—
I see them in ships and hallways and night skies
and I paint them huge and hang them on walls.
Toothy monsters wearing fur and chiton
live in soundless caverns
and holes under water, some are bacteria, others are titans.

SPIRIT IS ACTION. Truth is compassion.
A footprint of a wildcat in river sand
is a pool for a small toad while a raven
looks on and sings her quark song.
This is not a hell or haven
just sheer loveliness of the flowing middle.

ACTION IS PROTEIN. It is politics of flesh
and non-being, NOT nothing, not something,
here in the face. Here in the stomach and arms.
Just a transient truth, never a riddle
caught in the runes. Each being knows the tune,
like the giant seals enraged and high with battling.

BONES OF THE SABER TUSK TIGER IN ASPHALT;
now he's a statue in the park,
and bright in a boy's eye, with charms
tearing and ripping and screaming
in the black of the new moon.
The tiger is always there, free of the clinging mesh.

MOTILE POEMS LIKE FINGERS OR ROOT TIPS
seek nooks among strata
and in the bellies of cubs and children.
There is no place to crash.
Each crash flowers in warm light and sleet
beginning with quaking in mud of the vernal pool.

AMINO TRIGGERS IN SPACE; in ponds
on ripples, and among the moons of Saturn.
Everything burns for the eyes that will
come into being. The twisting shapes
are hunting their forms, the big ones
grow and shrink and in themselves are the answers.

WE ARE ACTIVITY — membrane edging under membrane
making trillions of children and larvae to feed
and be eaten. Pleistocene stretches backward
into infinity of nowhere, and is here with bones now and then.
The fern bends under the oak — fronds
of the once-gone future with life at the roots.

BELOW US IS STEADY AND SOLID,
stable, and stygian as the whirling
of four winds that hold up the water;
upon which floats earth with summers and glaciers,
and fossils in rocks and flesh
giving solidity to the causeless spark.

SOON ENOUGH a raft of logs floats over the river,
a tiny spot disappearing into fourteen
billion years suspended in the animal gel
of trillions of galaxies and countless stars.
Here the Pleistocene stinks and roars
in my shoulders and arms as I bow.

PERHAPS WE RETURN TO A POOL
— STEADY AND SOLID;
ready and already completed in fireworks
and lives and non-lives — thin and faint
as powerful odors stirring
my moment's soul in the mind of place.

NO MATTER — ANTI-MATTER — DARK ENERGY.
Imagined walls and rivers being solid real.
In the hole of nothingness — a pinprick —
where mastodons and antlered giraffes
and giant, meat-and-berry-hungry bears steal
through the uncarved block in their mammoth triumph.

WE HAVE THE JOY OF HERETICS
by simply being here, drinking from footsteps.
No pleasure, no shame, no guilt, just as life is.
Profoundly rich with enzymes and emotions,
instinctual lovers and haters, reasoning
a lovely rough trail through boundless seasons.

WE DID NOT CHOOSE IT — WE ARE HERE.
Putting bodies together without cause,
dying in pain, loving. Embryos with big eyes,
together in crowds make unities, sensing the trick.
Hearing snow plop softly from the pines
we can laugh and growl at the earth and sky.

PERFECT. Perfect. Perfect blotches
hanging together in undreamed causeless systems.
No time anywhere — like smears on fingers.
Inspiration changes tiny strings to thick
frequencies of matter. Hear the clatter
of a megatherium family by the water hole.

PERFECT PLATEAU BECOMING ODORS
AND TOUCHES, the jackrabbit munches
uncovered root tops by the old car.
We discover there are no laws
but the new one of the sizeless revolution,
seeking greater and greater, making ready to disappear.

I DID NOT KNOW THIS WAS NATURE.
One meaningless failure and triumph
after another: mussel cracks on a rock
on the belly of the floating otter.
There were white towers in the near distance;
open wounds coming to life, being there to heal.

THE BLANKET FLOWS OUT OF THE WINDOW
ON IT ARE YELLOW BANDS WOVEN
WITH RED BISON,
around it hummingbirds startle themselves
in the pollutants of the city's wind.
This, like moons of Saturn, and neurons, is real.

SOLID BLACKNESS ABOVE AND BELOW
holds the arrowheads of light
as the tips clang together. Sparks
or particles disappear from being
and happen together in nowhere.
It's simple as a colonial jellyfish and a cliff of chalk.

MUSIC BETWEEN the joining synapses of a larva
is almost as silent as a romance.
In the realms, past and to come,
are holy and unholy hungers
with no difference between them.
They are steps in what may be a dance.

FORESTS OF MOSS IN THE COLD STREAM
are islands in the middle of seas
and strands of invisible matter
wrapped around the ears of a squirrel.
Cold red eggs of salmon are tree-covered hills
and beings we endlessly conceive of.

BULK OF A DEAD SEA LION — DARK EYES OPEN
— a lump on the rocky beach smelling
like jellyfish rotting — a feast for the gulls.
Towers alight with electric dots
and their light blurs out in wet fog.
Growling of traffic and consciousness flows in the park.

THE DESERT IS ALIVE with mice, pumas, peyote,
sexual hungers of night flowers and sniffing bats
while the organelles of mitochondria
open their doors emptying out thoughts
of bodhisattvas and energy, broken and unbroken.
Galore! With stars and moon in a cozy gel.

THE FIR FEELS THE SOLSTICE, alive as a cracked stone
and a future comet reflected in waves.
All is here, is stable, and is hulls
and chaff blowing in wind and breezes
to settle into rock gorges
and interstitial, ciliated, hungry pebbles.

SENSE HORIZONTALLY, ASPIRE VERTICALLY
— AGNOSIA. A movie in a billion
modes of perception floats on a sheaf of mercury
flowing over the lip of non-beginning.
Consciousness like the tiniest dream
of the smallest imagining was never here.

KEATS, DIRAC, DIONYSIUS THE AREOPAGITE,
and Dogen know some of that and Sesshu hurled
it out in a splash of ink. Each stream
drinks up space. Huge condors
hover in bodies of the carrion-quarry they tear
from shadows and ribs on the ground and in the sky.

TRUMPETS, CYMBALS, WARM GRASS,
ROAR OF A MOTORCYCLE
mingle with hormones and glaciers
and eyes half-closed, feeling
the invention of a newly begotten memory.
This is perfect, in the middle between light and dark.

LEATHER, QUARTZ AND CINNAMON,
renegade rebels from sublimated education
shrink the size of the nervous system
as lungs and gonads grow
and more stately roaring moves with the tones
and bumping together of luck, chance, and hunger.

DISSOLUTION IS A PRIVILEGE,
is the final safe nest of nothing
like a small pine burning in a windy barranca.
Quarks and spotted butterflies flutter in squadrons
with no meaning for their knowledge
but a fleshy searching for a partly known liberation.

HAIL PLANARIAN!
Eyed, flat, dark worm
in the stream. Cousin, dear dragon, cousin
of lions and gravity. Free to free yourself
with sub-beings going to learn it again,
chilly as a comet. Four ravens passing over
quark your praises while Realm giants hunt in the bay trees.

SWEET WARM AND ODOROUS
IN THE AUTUMN SUN,
fields of mown yellow grass glint back
the barricade of stars that they support.
Herds of antelope and camels in all of their beauty,
and hoofprint trails left in mud are enough to atone.

BLACKER THAN BLACK, BLUE-BLACK
— A MIRROR REFLECTING REDS —
is the threat imagined in a brutal ending
and from it gleams warm light free of a cause.
Light in black, black in light, not a fact or a duty
but the flashing sides of waves where otters swim.

SCREAMS AND FLAMES OVER THE HORIZON
are delusions of Billy the Kid and large-minded
hunters tracking through snow. Scratches of claws
and prints lead them on into gut, muscle, and bones.
On the edge of stars cities are born —
we live with less than thoughts and a weaponed limb.

CREAK OF EUCALYPTUS BOUGHS over gentle ivy.
Here we are always. Hear the language birds are sending;
the smell of it rises in riches filling caves
under overturned roots in the whirring of near
and distant herds. These are our own lungs
made of stuff from nowhere and the empty glittering thrones.

THE PLATEAU IS A POINT,
THE MASK OF A DIMENSION,
that is shuffled realms, showing creatures
of non-consciousness. Bigger than ever,
tinier, thoughtful. Genius dreaming
mountains of heavy solid reason
perfect without lesion.

THE MASK IS ENFORCED BY ENSOCIALIZATION
OF PERCEPTIONS
that wither in passing, inspiring Marcuse
and Whitehead and the black flashes of light
from the eye
of a chipmunk. Hungry!
It is all hungry and full and growing in all directions.
Each selection is the mime and double of everything.

SEPTEMBER BLACKBERRIES ARE FREE.
Free as the conversation of ravens
on the shoulders of one who sits
beside a pool when the salmon jumps.
The lumps of experience on their fields
are stilled into synaptic inertia and streaming.

THERE ARE STILL BLOSSOMS
of wild cherries, chrysanthemums, psychedelic salvia,
serpentine strata, and slag by the factories.
The roarings of huge creatures are blossoms
as are a miniature primate, a Dire wolf,
and a jaguarundi crossing a trail by the ocean.

CONDENSATION FALLS PATTERING ON LEAVES.
Densifications are matter transmuting matter
back into the cavern of solid nothingness
and it falls over the heads, and the trails,
and sleek raw dreams at the lips of the precipice.
Sometimes there is the imagined memory of a quiet rattle.

MACHINE GUNS COMMUNICATE BULLETS
— what more is there to invent? —
and is inspired chatter and shapely babble of imagination.
Deathly tainted dust settles here and there
in the nests of pregnant rodents, and the fields
of comets, and a redwood tree with a rose in its shadow.

BOMBS ARE SYMBOLS OF MEAT THOUGHTS
in the dimunitive vastness of Pleistocene tundra.
Thundering is much more lovely, and a golden bolt
lights up the spotted cushions we lie upon.
It's here in the blending of dawn and sunset
where armadillos and mountains are walking boulders.

FACES OF MALEVOLENCE AND FOLLY
STARE FROM THE WALLS
and who could not love them for their innocence?
They are painted with the roars and whistles
of living voices rolling over on a wheel,
turning and laughing in the long fall to beginning.

THE FLEECE MOVING IN THE BREEZE
BY THE FIRE IS LOVELY.
While lying there watching, all things are seen
in the nothingness of their spinning.
Odors from the yellow-blond fur tips
are just eyebrows holding unconfined worlds.

WE ARE OLD WOLVES,
INDIANS, CREATURES.
All else is a lie, like all lives,
as lovely and smooth as the waves we float in.
We are perfect, imperfect, rising and sinking ships
in the smell of burning pine and the mask that unfurls.

ETERNITY BECOMES BROWN-GOLD
FOR AN INSTANT.
We are stoned as we are always stoned
listening to cries of uncreated fields of silence.
Nothing like this is ever known before.
Cobwebs between comets and mammals
and lines of the suns are massive doors.

TIME IS THE LONG WAY BACK
and the future is dangerously filled
with loving and dreams and concussions on floors
of what is imagined and inspired, solid real.
Ugliness is as naked as beauty with lips
of newly discovered colors resting in metals and bones.

IGNORANCE, LIKE INFORMATION, IS A LEVER
puffing up, draining the present, future, and past
in realms that know all of nothingness.
Scarlet is the influence of sugar and dream flowers,
where incense burns, flown over by pelican flights
in the uncanny stench of unimagined musk.

THE BODY'S ODORS—THE BERRY'S ODORS
are one thing in the sweetness of non-beginning.
Just where the mussel shell cracks on the stone,
in the storms that are heard and unheard,
pines and tamarisks are beings of solidity
rising up, with water and gases and sun, out of nowhere.

THE MASS OF INFORMATION WHITES OUT,
dissolving the future and making life for more.
Just as all was gone, not even sleeping before.
It is here in the dusk with nothing to last
and bright as newborn, writhing plankton
this cannot be, nothing was here before.

RAINBOW AGAINST WHITE—PROJECTED ON BLACK,
or a moon-bow of ivory telling the time
that will come to be tangled in roots of cress
in the brook. This canny voiceless whisper
powers all galaxies as the water strider
skims on the Technicolor pool.

THE SELVES FLYING THROUGH
THE BODY HAVE FACES
as they often have been seen before,
meeting and bowing and passing through another
in clusters like gnats in the setting sun
and built into cliffs of momentary stars.

THEY STREAM WITH TAILS OF COLORS.
They reach ahead with the complex blackness
of a worm. Sensing all. The all in nothing
at the edge of the tundra, at the foot
of the glaciers where the dwarves storm
in the clanging of singing and cymbals of dusk.

SENSATION MAY PRECEDE INFORMATION
as it always has when real walls
collapse at the strike of a flaming sword
made of buds and flowers and eyes of dimensions.
It is a finale and newborn creation of form
that the glory of each moment's shape absorbs.

WE DIVE BOTH DOWN AND OUTWARD
through eleven dimensions that curl one
into another and fan their pack
of endless cards. Each with a picture
of an otter, raven, giant desert tortoise,
city with towers flaming, and the trail of the Middle Way.

SOLIDITY AND VIBRATION
are not the same. There's nothing of either
in the path cleared in snowbanks
by the sweep of the mammoth's tusks.
It's a bridge for a stream, no hurdle,
no signs for trucks, no sounds, no words.

UNEXPECTED PROFILES AND FACES
disappear before their birth out of nowhere
blinking out so the Middle Way may appear,
for the middle is stone, fire, space and thought.
And the jay wipes her beak, turning
her shiny eye to the monkey flower and sound of cymbals.

THE BRAMBLE TANGLE
IS A MOVING SCULPTURE
at the foot of the fall where the stones drop.
There is nothing to stop or move backwards
in the shifting. It is creasing and uplifting.
The light of endless rivers of stars makes no change.

DRAGONS OF SPACE AND MATTER
— all matter when the cave of dark energy
turns inside out and the limitless
swirl turns faces in every direction, with no realms to arrange.
How tender to touch is the ripe, white-purple
cluster of elderberries where the deer mice run.

FALSE PERCEPTIONS MIMIC THE REAL
— A COVER. There is only one heart to the matter
and it disappears, drifting, not drifting,
but never gone. Tentatively locked in the taste
and the size of the conscious wings. Emeralds, rubies,
turquoise, and a pine needle are the measure of things.

THE BODY MAY BE DIAGRAMMED
WITH COLORS AND ODORS,
where a cub sits beckoning to a mother,
or a child sings to an old man who listens
by a glistening, popping and cracking fire.
There it is after crossing the river in the black and golden waste.

THERE IS A FIRE AND TRAJECTORIES
OF ENERGIES bare of knowing or thought
where black inferno meets meat in bliss.
Raindrops tap on the windshield with no fury
just muffled kindness in the fog of skies.
Here beings (all is beings) mutely perceive themselves first.

BEYOND THE MASK OF THE POINT ARE
TRILLIONIC INTERLOCKED CONSTELLATIONS
guided by no laws but the paths of capillaries,
streams tinkling in blackness, and the coyote's sky-confession
to dawn, as the red-silver sun flares
a hole in the sky wall and the tiger screams, battling in asphalt-tar.

PLEASURES ARE NOT RELATIVE BUT ACTUAL
— BLACKBERRIES, SEA LIONS, TENDRILS,
ambrosia — they drench hell realms.
The shapes of masses of galaxies, stems
of flowers, and solid stuff of flesh
is proportionless, limitless in every world — making storms.

PERCEPTIONS ARE HERETIC
— THEY NEGATE ABSENCE —
just as all things are dissolved of forms.
Glaciers of the Pleistocene with streams
running from their star- and sun-flaring cliffs
blow horns in ice caverns, and tundras begin to crack.

ABSENCE IS LACK OF PERCEPTION.

THE MUSSEL SHELL CRACKS ON THE ROCK.

WAVES OF WATER AND PROTOPLASM...

COYOTE SHIT—THE TAJ MAHAL...

WINGED TIGERS ENCASED IN TRANSPARENT SILVER...

MY WHISKERS—THE WOLF'S BEARD.

TO ROBERT CREELEY
for Penelope

Farewell Bob, from your syncopated
whip-crack of Miles Davis
and your de Kooning stroke
to your vision of the paintings
in the Cro-Magnon caves. Goodbye, poet,
touch my shoulder as you touched it.
You were my first literary friend
and you were a drunken and demonic adventurer
who changed to become a father and husband
in this world and to the writing realms
and dimensions of spoken genius.
From you we learned grace and accuracy
of the gestures of the voice
and to flex syllables
upon the breath of muscular intelligence.

Outrider of energy,
guardian of poetry's dark serious laugh,
today in the sun the fiddleneck ferns unclasp
and the first mariposa tulip
opens in the field.
Inspired by your shadow
none of us will yield.